Faith

The Grace of Faith

*Now faith is the substance of things hoped for,
the evidence of things not seen.
For by it the elders obtained a good testimony.*

HEBREWS 11:1–2

The grace of faith is the substance of things hoped for. Faith and hope go together, and the same things that are the object of our hope are the object of our faith. We are of a firm persuasion and expectation that God will perform all that He has promised to us in Christ. Believers in the exercise of faith are filled with joy unspeakable and full of glory. Faith is the evidence of things not seen. Faith demonstrates to the eye of the mind the reality of those things that cannot be discerned by the eye of the body. It is designed to serve the believer instead of sight and to be to the soul all that the senses are to the body.

True faith is an old grace and has the best plea to antiquity: It is not a new invention, a modern fancy. The eldest and best men that ever were in the world were believers. They were an honor to their faith, and their faith was an honor to them. It started them doing the things that were of good report.

Converting Grace

For by grace you have been saved through faith,
and that not of yourselves; it is the gift of God,
not of works, lest anyone should boast.

EPHESIANS 2:8–9

There is no room for any man's boasting of his own abilities and power; or as though he had done anything that might deserve such immense favors from God. God Himself is the author of this great and happy change. Love is His inclination to do good to us, considered simply as creatures: Mercy respects us as apostate and miserable creatures. That love of God is great love, and that mercy of His is rich mercy. Every converted sinner is a saved sinner. The grace that saves them is the free, undeserved goodness and favor of God, and He saves them not by the works of the law, but through faith in Christ Jesus. Both that faith and that salvation are the gifts of God.

Grace in the soul is a new life in the soul. Grace unlocks and opens all and enlarges the soul. A regenerate sinner becomes a living soul, being born of God. It is in Him that we live. We who were buried are raised up. When He raised Christ from the dead, He in effect raised up all believers together with Him, and when He placed Him at His right hand in heavenly places, He advanced and glorified them in and with Him.

The Author of Our Faith

Therefore we also,
since we are surrounded by so great a cloud
of witnesses, let us lay aside every weight,
and the sin which so easily ensnares us,
and let us run with endurance the race
that is set before us, looking unto Jesus,
the author and finisher of our faith, who for the joy
that was set before Him endured the cross,
despising the shame, and has sat down at the right hand
of the throne of God.

HEBREWS 12:1–2

Christians have a race to run. This race is set before them; it is marked out for them both by the Word of God and the examples of the faithful servants of God, that cloud of witnesses that encompasses the faithful. This race must be run with patience and perseverance. Faith and patience are the conquering graces and therefore must always be cultivated.

Christians have a greater example to encourage them than any who have been mentioned before. Jesus, the author and finisher of their faith, is the great leader and precedent of our faith. He is the finisher of grace and of the work of faith in the souls of His people, and He is the judge and the rewarder of their faith.

We must look to Jesus and set Him continually before us as our example. We must consider Him and meditate much upon Him. We shall find that as His sufferings far exceeded ours, so His patience far excels ours.

There is a tendency in the best of us to grow weary and to faint under our trials and afflictions. The best way to prevent this is to look to Jesus.

The Only Way to Salvation

Then he [the jailer] called for a light. . .and fell down
trembling before Paul and Silas. . .and said,
"Sirs, what must I do to be saved?" So they said,
"Believe on the Lord Jesus Christ, and you will be saved,
you and your household."

ACTS 16:29–31

Paul and Silas gave the jailer the same directions they did to others, the sum of the whole gospel, the covenant of grace in a few words: "Believe on the Lord." Not only would the jailer be rescued from eternal ruin but also brought to eternal life and blessedness. Though a persecutor, his heinous transgressions would all be forgiven, and his hard, embittered heart softened and sweetened by the grace of Christ. We must approve the method God has taken of reconciling the world to Himself by a mediator and accept Christ as He is offered to us. This is the only sure way to salvation. There is no other way of salvation than by Christ. . . . It is the gospel that is to be preached to every creature.

The apostles proceeded to instruct him and his family in the doctrine of Christ, speaking the Word to all who were in his house. Masters of families should take care that all under their charge partake of the means of knowledge and grace and that the word of the Lord is spoken to them, for the souls of the poorest servants are as precious as those of their masters and are bought with the same price.

The jailer and his family were immediately baptized. The Spirit of grace worked such a strong faith in them that Paul and Silas knew by the Spirit that a work of God had been done in them.

If

*Jesus said to him, "If you can believe,
all things are possible to him who believes."*

MARK 9:23

"If You can do anything, have compassion on us and
help us," begged the father of the possessed child (v.
22). The answer Christ gave to this plea checked the
weakness of the father's faith. The sufferer put it upon
Christ's power, but Christ turned it upon him and
made the man question his own faith and would have
him impute any disappointment to a lack of faith on
his own part. He graciously encouraged the strength
of his desire: "All things are possible to him who believes the almighty power of God, to which all things
are possible." In dealing with Christ, much is put on
our believing, and very much is promised to it. Can you
believe? Do you dare to believe? If you can, it is possible that your hard heart may be softened, your spiritual diseases may be cured, and that, weak as you are,
you may be able to hold out to the end.

The poor man cried out, "Lord, I believe; my cure
shall not be prevented by the want of faith. Lord, I
believe." He adds a prayer for grace to enable him
more firmly to rely on Christ to save: "Help my unbelief." Those who complain of unbelief must look up to
Christ for grace to help them against it, and His grace
shall be sufficient for them. "Help out what is want-
ing in my faith with Your grace, the strength of which
is perfected in our weakness."

The Power of Faith

*"I say to you, if you have faith as a mustard seed,
you will say to this mountain,
'Move from here to there,'
and it will move;
and nothing will be impossible for you."*

MATTHEW 17:20

Our Lord Jesus takes this occasion to show us the power of faith. Some make the comparison to refer to the quality of the mustard seed, which is, when bruised, sharp and penetrating. "If you have an active, growing faith, not dead, flat, or insipid, you will not be baffled." But it rather refers to the quantity: "If you had but a grain of true faith, though so little that it were like that which is the least of all seeds, you would do wonders." The faith required here is that which had for its object that particular revelation by which Christ gave His disciples power to work miracles in His name. It was a faith in this revelation that they were defective in. Perhaps their Master's absence might occasion some doubts concerning their power to do this. It is good for us to be diffident of ourselves and our own strength, but it is displeasing to Christ when we distrust any power derived from or granted by Him.

If you have ever so little of this faith, in sincerity you shall say to the mountain, "Move." Nothing shall be impossible for you. They distrusted the power they had received, and so they failed. An active faith can move mountains—not of itself, but in the virtue of a divine power engaged by a divine promise.

Spiritual Warfare

*Taking the shield of faith with which you will be able
to quench all the fiery darts of the wicked one.*

EPHESIANS 6:16

Christians must see that they are stouthearted. Those
who have so many battles to fight and who, on their
way to heaven, must dispute every pass with the sword,
have need of a great deal of courage. A soldier can be
ever so well armed, but if he does not have a good
heart, his armor will stand him in little stead. Spiritual
strength and courage are very necessary for our spiritual warfare. We do not have sufficient strength on our
own; all our sufficiency is from God. In His strength
we must go forth and go on. We must call in grace and
help from heaven to enable us to do what we cannot
do alone.

Faith is all in all to us in an hour of temptation. The
breastplate secures the vitals, but with a shield we may
turn every way. Faith is like a shield, a sort of universal
defense. Our enemy the devil endeavors to make us
wicked. His temptations are called fiery darts, an allu-
sion to poisonous darts. Violent temptations, by which
the soul is set on fire, are the darts that Satan shoots at
us. Faith is the shield with which we must quench these
darts, that they may not hit us, or at least that they may
not hurt us.

Faith Heals

Jesus turned around, and when He saw her He said,
"Be of good cheer, daughter;
your faith has made you well."
And the woman was made well from that hour.

MATTHEW 9:22

This woman's disease was of such a nature that her modesty would not allow her to speak openly to Christ for a cure, as others did, but she believed Him to have such an overflowing fullness of healing virtue that the very touch of His garment would cure her. Christ allowed this bashful patient to steal a cure unknown to anyone else, though she could not think to do it unknown to Him. Now she was well content to be gone, for she had what she came for. But Christ was not willing to let her go. The triumphs of her faith must be to her praise and honor. He turned and discovered her. He called her "daughter," for He spoke to her with the tenderness of a father, and He bid her to be of good cheer, telling her that her faith had made her whole. Her bodily cure was the fruit of faith, of her faith, and that made it a happy, comfortable cure indeed.

Prayer

Pray Always

*Praying always with all prayer
and supplication in the Spirit,
being watchful to this end with all perseverance
and supplication for all the saints.*

EPHESIANS 6:18

Prayer must buckle on all the other parts of our Christian armor. We must join prayer with all these graces, and we must pray always. Not as though we were to do nothing else but pray, for there are other duties that are to be done in their place and season, but we should keep up constant times of prayer. We must pray on all occasions. We must intermix prayers with other duties and with common business. Though set and solemn prayer may sometimes be unseasonable, yet pious prayers can never be so. We must pray with all prayer and supplications, with all kinds of prayer. We must pray in the Spirit, by the grace of God's good Spirit. We must watch, endeavoring to keep our hearts in a praying frame and taking all occasions for the duty. This we must do with all perseverance. We must continue in it as long as we live in the world. And we must pray with supplication, not only for ourselves, but for all saints. None are so much saints, and in so good a condition in this world, that they do not need our prayers, and they ought to have them.

A Prayer-Hearing God

"Ask, and it will be given to you;
seek, and you will find; knock,
and it will be opened to you."

MATTHEW 7:7

Here is a precept in three words: *Ask, seek, knock.* That is, in one word, "Pray, pray, and pray again." Ask, as a beggar asks alms. Those who would be rich in grace must take to the poor trade of begging, and they shall find it a thriving trade. Ask; represent your wants and burdens to God. Ask, as a traveler asks the way; to pray is to inquire of God. Seek, as if seeking for a thing of value that you have lost. Seek by prayer. Knock, as he who desires to enter into the house knocks at the door. Sin has shut and barred the door against us, but by prayer we knock: Lord, Lord, open to us. Christ knocks at our door and allows us to knock at His, which is a favor we do not allow to common beggars. Seeking and knocking imply something more than asking and praying. We must not only ask but seek; we must second our prayers with our endeavors. We must, by the appointed means, seek for that which we ask for, else we tempt God. We must not only ask, but knock; we must come to God's door, must ask importunately; we not only pray, but plead and watch with God.

There is a promise added: Our labor in prayer, if we do indeed labor at it, shall not be in vain. When God finds a praying heart, He will be found a prayer-hearing God. He will give you an answer of peace.

Where Do I Pray?

"But you, when you pray, go into your room,
and when you have shut your door,
pray to your Father who is in the secret place;
and your Father who sees in secret
will reward you openly."

MATTHEW 6:6

Instead of praying publicly, go into some place of privacy and retirement. Isaac went into the field, Christ to a mountain, Peter to the housetop. No place is wrong if it answers the end. Yet if the circumstances are such that we cannot possibly avoid being taken notice of, we must not therefore neglect the duty, lest the omission is a greater scandal than the observation of it.

Instead of doing it to be seen of men, pray to your Father who is in secret. The Pharisees prayed to men, not God. Pray to God, and let that be enough. Pray to Him as a father, as your Father, ready to hear and answer, graciously inclined to pity, help, and comfort you. Pray to your Father who is in secret. He is there in your room when no one else is there, especially close to you in whatever you call on Him for.

Your Father sees in secret. There is not a secret, sudden breathing after God that He does not observe. He will reward you openly. They have their reward who pray openly, and you shall not lose yours for praying in secret. It is called a reward, but it is of grace, not of debt. Sometimes secret prayers are rewarded openly in this world by unusual answers to them, which manifests God's praying people in the consciences of their adversaries.

Prayers As Praise and Thanksgiving

"In this manner, therefore, pray:
Our Father in heaven, hallowed be Your name."

MATTHEW 6:9

Because we know not what to pray for, Jesus helps our infirmities by putting words into our mouths. Not that we are tied to the use of this form only, as if this were necessary to the consecrating of our other prayers. We are told to pray in this manner, with these words, or to this effect. Yet, without doubt, it is very good to use it as a form, and it is a pledge of the communion of saints, having been used by the church in all ages. It is used acceptably when it is used with understanding and without vain repetition.

Prayer is a form of praise and thanksgiving. The best pleading with God is praise. Praise is the way to obtain mercy, since it qualifies us to receive it. We praise God and give Him glory, not because He needs it—He is praised by a world of angels—but because He deserves it. Praise is the work and happiness of heaven; and all who would go to heaven must begin their heaven now. It becomes us to be copious in praising God. A true saint never thinks he can speak honorably enough of God.

Prayers for All

Therefore I exhort first of all that supplications, prayers, intercessions, and giving of thanks be made for all men.

1 TIMOTHY 2:1

This is Paul's charge to Christians to pray for all men in general, and particularly for all in authority. Paul does not send Timothy any prescribed form of prayer. Paul thought it enough to give them general heads; they, having the Scripture to direct them in prayer poured out on them, needed no further directions. The disciples of Christ must be praying people. There must be prayers for ourselves in the first place. This is implied here. We must also pray for all men. Though the kings at this time were heathens, yet they must pray for them. We must give thanks for them, pray for their welfare and for the welfare of their kingdoms, that in the peace thereof, we may have peace. The summit of the ambition of good Christians is to lead a quiet and peaceable life. We cannot expect to be kept quiet and peaceable unless we keep in all godliness and honesty. Here we have our duty as Christians summed up in two words: godliness, that is, the right worshiping of God; and honesty, that is, good conduct toward all men. These two must go together. Christians are to be men much given to prayer. In our prayers we are to have a generous concern for others as well as for ourselves; we are to pray for all men and to give thanks for all men.

Let Your Requests
Be Made Known

Be anxious for nothing,
but in everything by prayer and supplication,
with thanksgiving, let your requests be made known to God;
and the peace of God, which surpasses all understanding,
will guard your hearts and minds through Christ Jesus.

PHILIPPIANS 4:6–7

A caution against disquieting, perplexing care: "Be anxious for nothing." Avoid anxious care and distracting thought in the wants and difficulties of life. It is the duty and interest of Christians to live without care. There is a care of diligence that is our duty, but there is a care of distrust which is our sin and folly.

The author recommends constant prayer. "In everything by prayer and supplication, with thanksgiving, let your requests be made known to God." We must pray for every emergency, "in everything by prayer." When anything burdens our spirits, we must ease our minds by prayer; when our affairs are perplexed or distressed, we must seek direction and support. We must join thanksgiving with our prayers and supplications. We must not only seek supplies of good but have receipts of mercy. Prayer is the offering up of our desires to God. Not that God needs to be told either our wants or desires, but He would like to hear of them from us. The effect of this will be the peace of God. The peace of God is a greater good than can be sufficiently valued or duly expressed. This peace will keep our hearts and minds through Jesus Christ. It will keep us from sinning under our troubles and from sinking under them.

Bible Study

The Power of Scripture

For the word of God is living and powerful. . .
sharper than any two-edged sword. . .
and is a discerner of the thoughts and intents of the heart.

HEBREWS 4:12

The Word of God gives us great help in attaining the peace we need. It is living, very lively and active in seizing the conscience of the sinner, in cutting him to the heart, and in comforting him and binding up the wounds of the soul. It is powerful. It convinces powerfully, converts powerfully, and comforts powerfully. It is powerful enough to batter down Satan's kingdom and set up the kingdom of Christ upon the ruins. It is sharper than any two-edged sword. It will enter where no other sword can and make a more critical dissection. It pierces to the dividing asunder of the soul and the spirit, the soul and its habitual prevailing temper. It makes a soul that has been proud for a long time humble, a soul that has been perverse meek and obedient. This sword divides between the joints and the marrow. It can make men willing to undergo the sharpest operation for the mortifying of sin. It is a discerner of the thoughts and intents of the heart. The Word will turn the sinner inside out and let him see all that is in his heart.

God's Word Helps Us Grow

As newborn babes, desire the pure milk of the word,
that you may grow thereby.

1 PETER 2:2

The best Christians need to be cautioned and warned against the worst sins. They are only sanctified in part and are still liable to temptations. Our best services toward God will neither please Him nor profit us if we are not conscientious in our duties to men. One sin not laid aside will hinder our spiritual profit and everlasting welfare.

The apostle, like a wise physician, goes on to direct us to wholesome food, that we may grow thereby. The duty exhorted to is a strong and constant desire for the Word of God. This milk of the Word must be sincere, not adulterated by the mixtures of men. A new life requires suitable food. Infants desire common milk, and their desires toward it are fervent and frequent. Such must Christians' desires be for the Word of God, that they may grow thereby. Strong desires and affections to the Word of God are a sure evidence of a person's being born again. Growth and improvement in wisdom and grace are the desire of every Christian. The Word of God does not leave a man as it finds him.

Day and Night

*"This Book of the Law shall not depart from your mouth,
but you shall meditate in it day and night."*

JOSHUA 1:8

Joshua was to conform himself in everything to the law of God and make this his rule. God puts the Book of the Law into Joshua's hand, and he is charged to meditate on it day and night. If ever any man's business might have excused him from meditation and other acts of devotion, one would think Joshua's might at this time. It was a great trust that was lodged in his hands; the care of it was enough to fill him, and yet he must find time and thoughts for meditation. He was not to let the Word depart out of his mouth; that is, all his orders to the people must be consistent with the law of God, and on all occasions he must speak according to this rule. There was no need to make new laws, but that good thing that was committed to him he must carefully and faithfully keep. He must observe to do according to the law. Joshua was a man of great power and authority, yet he himself must be under command and do as he is bidden. No man's dignity or dominion sets him above the law of God.

Joshua must observe the checks of conscience, the hints of providence, and all the advantages of opportunity. He must not turn from the Word in his own practice or in any act of government. He must be strong and courageous. Finally, Joshua is assured that following this way will make him, and those who follow him, prosperous.

That We Might Have Hope

For whatever things were written before
were written for our learning, that we through. . .
the Scriptures might have hope.

ROMANS 15:4

That which is written of Christ is written for our learning. He has left us an example. The example of Christ is recorded for our imitation. That which is written in the Scriptures of the Old Testament is written for our learning. What happened to the Old Testament saints happened to them as an example. They were written for our use and benefit. We must therefore labor not only to understand the literal meaning of the Scripture, but to learn out of it that which will do us good. Practical observations are more necessary than critical expositions. The Scripture was written that we might know what to hope for from God. Now the way of attaining this hope is through patience and comfort of the Scripture. Patience and comfort suppose trouble and sorrow; such is the lot of the saints in this world. But both these befriend that hope that is the life of our souls. Patience works experience, and experience hope, which maketh not ashamed. The more patience we exercise under troubles, the more hopefully we may look through our troubles. Nothing is more destructive to hope than impatience. And the comfort of the Scriptures, that comfort that springs from the Word of God, is likewise a great stay to hope, since it is an earnest in hand for the good hoped for.

Devotion and Commitment

Fruitful and Faithful Disciples

"If you keep My commandments,
you will abide in My love,
just as I have kept My Father's commandments
and abide in His love."

JOHN 15:10

Jesus tells His disciples that if they bring forth much fruit and continue in His love, He will continue to rejoice in them as He had done. Fruitful and faithful disciples are the joy of the Lord Jesus. It is the will of Christ that His disciples should constantly and continually rejoice in Him. The joy of those who abide in Christ's love is a continual feast.

They were to show their love of Him by keeping His commandments. "If you keep My commandments, you will abide in My love." The promise is that you shall live in the love of Jesus as in a dwelling place, at home in Christ's love; as in a resting place, at ease in Christ's love; as in a stronghold, safe in it. The condition of this promise is "If you keep My commandments." The disciples were to keep Christ's commandments not only by a constant conformity to themselves, but by a faithful delivery of them to others; they were to keep them as trustees.

To induce them to keep His commandments, He urges His own example: "As I have kept My Father's commandments and abide in His love." In other words: "You are My friends if you do whatever I command you." Only those who prove themselves His obedient servants will be Christ's faithful friends. Universal obedience to Christ is the only acceptable obedience.

Rich in the Faith

Listen, my beloved brethren:
Has God not chosen the poor of this world
to be rich in faith and heirs of the kingdom which
He promised to those who love Him?

JAMES 2:5

Respect of persons is a heinous sin, because it shows us directly contrary to God. God has made those heirs of a kingdom whom you make of no reputation. Many of the poor of this world are the chosen of God. Their being God's chosen does not prevent their being poor; their being poor does not at all prejudice the evidence of their being chosen. God designed to recommend His holy religion not by the external advantages of gaiety and pomp, but by its intrinsic worth. . . .

Many poor of the world are rich in faith; thus the poorest may become rich. It is expected from those who have wealth that they be rich in good works, but it is expected from the poor in the world that they be rich in faith. Believing Christians are heirs of a kingdom. . . . Where any are rich in faith, there will divine love also be. We read of the crown promised to those who love God. We find there is a kingdom, too. And as the crown is a crown of life, so the kingdom will be an everlasting kingdom. After such considerations as these, the charge is cutting indeed. Respecting persons on account of their riches or outward figure is shown to be a very great sin because of the mischiefs that are owing to worldly wealth and greatness. This will make your sin appear exceedingly sinful and foolish, in setting up that which tends to pull you down and to dishonor that worthy name by which you are called.

Commit Your Works to the Lord

Commit your works to the LORD,
and your thoughts will be established.

PROVERBS 16:3

In short, man purposes. He has the freedom of thought and the freedom of will given to him. Let him form his projects and plan his schemes as he thinks best but, after all, God disposes. Man cannot go on with his business without the assistance and blessing of God, who made man's mouth and teaches us what we shall say.

We are all apt to be partial in judging ourselves. The judgment of God concerning us is according to truth: He weighs the spirits in a just and unerring balance, knows what is in us, and passes judgment on us accordingly, and by His judgment we will stand or fall.

The only way to have our thoughts established is to commit our works to the Lord. The great concerns of our souls must be committed to the grace of God. All our outward concerns must be committed to the providence of God and to the sovereign, wise, and gracious disposal of that providence. Roll your works upon the Lord; roll the burden of your care from yourself onto God.

The Work of Our Hands

*And let the beauty of the LORD our God be upon us,
and establish the work of our hands for us;
yes, establish the work of our hands.*

PSALM 90:17

Let Your work appear upon Your servants; let it appear that You have wrought upon us, to bring us home to Yourself and to fit us for Yourself. Let Your work appear, and in it Your glory will appear to us and those who shall come after us. Perhaps in this prayer the Israelites distinguish between themselves and their children, for so God distinguished in His late message to them (Numbers 14:23–29). "Your carcasses shall fall in this wilderness, but your little ones will I bring into Canaan."

"Lord," they say, "let Your work appear on us, to reform us, and bring us to a better temper, and then let Your glory appease to our children, in performing the promise to them which we have forfeited." Let it appear that God favors us. Let the grace of God in us and the light of our good works make our faces shine, and let divine consolations put gladness into our hearts and a luster upon our countenances, and that also will be the beauty of the Lord upon us. "Establish the work of our hands for us." God's working upon us does not discharge us from using our utmost endeavors in serving Him and working out our salvation. But when we have done all, we must wait upon God for the success.

All in Vain?

"Then I said, 'I have labored in vain,
I have spent my strength
for nothing and in vain; yet surely my just reward is
with the LORD, and my work with my God.'"

ISAIAH 49:4

Isaiah spoke of the discouragement he had met with at his first setting out. "Then I said, with a sad heart, I have labored in vain; those who were careless, and strangers to God, are so still. I have called and they have refused; I have stretched out my hands to a gainsaying people." Jeremiah was tempted to stop his work for the same reasons. It is the complaint of many a faithful minister that has not loitered, but labored, not spared, but spent his strength and himself with it. They will not repent and believe.

He comforts himself under this discouragement with this consideration, that it was the cause of God in which he was engaged: "Yet surely my judgment is with the Lord, who is the judge of all, and my work with my God, whose servant I am." His comfort may be the comfort of all faithful ministers when they see little success of their labors. They are with God and for God; they are on His side and workers together with Him. "He knows the way that I take; my judgment is with the Lord, to determine whether I have not delivered my soul and left the blood of those who perish on their own heads." Though the labor is in vain, if he is faithful, the Lord will justify him and bear him out, though men condemn him. The work is with the Lord, to give them success according to His purpose, in His own way and time.

Fulfilling Your Ministry

But you be watchful in all things, endure afflictions,
do the work of an evangelist, fulfill your ministry.

2 TIMOTHY 4:5

Paul reminded Timothy of his duty before God: 1. To preach the Word. This is ministers' business. It is not their own notions and fancies that they are to preach but the pure, plain Word of God. 2. To urge what he preached: "Be instant in season and out of season, reprove, rebuke, exhort; do this work with all fervency of spirit." 3. He must tell people of their faults and endeavor, by dealing plainly with them, to bring them to repentance. 4. He must direct, encourage, and quicken those who began well. He must do so very patiently. He must do it rationally, not with passion, but with doctrine. Teach them the truth as it is in Jesus, and this will be a means both to reclaim them from evil and bring them to good. 5. He must watch in all things. "Watch to thy work; watch against the temptations of Satan; watch over the souls of those who are committed to your charge." 6. He must count upon afflictions and endure them. 7. He must remember his office and discharge its duties. The office of the evangelist was, as the apostles' deputy, to water the churches the apostles planted. 8. He must fulfill his ministry, performing all the parts of his office with diligence and care. The best way to make full proof of our ministry is to fulfill it, to fill it up in all its parts with proper work.

Intimacy
with God

Spiritual Joys

"Therefore you now have sorrow;
but I will see you again and your heart will rejoice,
and your joy no one will take from you."

JOHN 16:22

Here Jesus tells the disciples of the sorrow they were soon to experience. "You now have sorrow, because I am leaving you." Christ's withdrawings are a just cause of grief to His disciples. When the sun sets, the sunflower will hang its head.

He, more largely than before, assures them of a return of joy. Three things recommend the joy. The cause of it is "I will see you again." Christ will graciously return to those who wait for Him. Men, when they are exalted, will scarcely look at their inferiors, but the exalted Jesus will visit His disciples. Christ's returns are returns of joy to all His disciples. The cordiality of His return is that "your heart will rejoice." Joy in the heart is solid and not flashy. It is secret, it is sweet, it is sure, and not easily broken in upon. The continuance of their joy: "Your joy no one will take from you." They would if they could, but they shall not prevail. Some understand Him to be speaking of the eternal joy of the glorified. Our joys on earth we may be robbed of by a thousand accidents, but heavenly joys are everlasting. I rather understand Him to be speaking of the spiritual joys of those who are sanctified. They could not rob them of their joy because they could not separate them from the love of Christ, and could not rob them of their God or of their treasure in heaven.

Our Source of Courage

*Wait on the LORD; be of good courage,
and He shall strengthen your heart;
wait, I say, on the LORD!*

PSALM 27:14

David expresses his dependence on God. "When I am helpless as every poor orphan who was left fatherless and motherless, then I know the Lord will take me up" (v. 10). He believed he would see the goodness of the Lord in the land of the living; and, if he had not done so, he would have fainted under his afflictions (v. 13). Those who walk by faith in the goodness of the Lord shall in due time walk in the sight of that goodness. It is his comfort, not so much that he will see the land of the living as that he will see the goodness of God in it, for that is the comfort of all creature comforts to a gracious soul. Heaven is that land that may truly be called the land of the living. This earth is the land of the dying. There is nothing like the believing hope of eternal life to keep us from fainting under all the calamities of this present time. In the meantime David says to himself or to his friends, "He shall strengthen your heart," shall sustain the spirit. In that strength, wait on the Lord by faith, and prayer, and a humble resignation to His will. "Wait, I say, on the Lord!" Whatever you do, do not become remiss in your attendance upon God. Those who wait on the Lord have reason to be of good courage.

Your Father's Good Pleasure

"Do not fear, little flock,
for it is your Father's good pleasure
to give you the kingdom."

LUKE 12:32

When we frighten ourselves with an apprehension of
evil to come, we concern ourselves with how to avoid
it, when after all perhaps it is only the creation of our
own imagination. Therefore "Do not fear, little flock,
for it is your Father's good pleasure to give you the
kingdom." This comfortable word we did not have in
Matthew. Christ's flock in this world is a little flock.
The church is a vineyard, a garden, a small spot, compared to the wilderness of this world. Though it is a
little flock, quite outnumbered by its enemies, yet it is
the will of Christ that they should not be afraid. "Fear
not, little flock, but see yourselves safe under the pro-
tection and conduct of the great and good shepherd."
God has a kingdom in store for all that belong to
Christ's little flock, a crown of glory (1 Peter 5:4). The
kingdom is given according to the good pleasure of the
Father: "It is your Father's good pleasure"; it is given
not as payment for a debt, but by grace. The believing
hopes and prospects of the kingdom should silence
and suppress the fears of Christ's little flock in this
world. "Fear no trouble; for, though it should come, it
shall not come between you and the kingdom." (That
is not an evil worth trembling at the thought of which
cannot separate us from the love of God.)

We Are Never Alone

Nevertheless I am continually with You;
You hold me by my right hand.
You will guide me with Your counsel,
and afterward receive me to glory.

PSALM 73:23–24

The psalmist admits his dependence on the grace of God. "Nevertheless I am continually with You," and in Your favor, "You hold me by my right hand." He had said, in the hour of temptation (v. 14), "All day long I have been plagued," but here he corrects himself for that passionate complaint. "Though God has chastened me, He has not cast me off. Notwithstanding all the crosses of my life, I have been continually with You." "Though God has sometimes written bitter things against me, yet He has still held me by my right hand to prevent my losing my way in the wildernesses through which I have walked." If He thus maintains the spiritual life, the promise of eternal life, we ought not to complain. "My feet were almost gone, and they would have quite gone, past recovery, but You held me by my right hand and so kept me from falling."

He encouraged himself to hope that the same God who had delivered him from this evil work would preserve him to His heavenly kingdom. . . . The psalmist would have paid dearly for following his own counsels in this temptation, and therefore resolves for the future to take God's advice. If God directs us in the way of our duty, He will afterward reconcile us to all the dark providences that now puzzle and perplex us, and ease us of the pain we have been put into by some threatening temptations.

Worship

Worship and Bow Down

Oh come, let us worship and bow down;
let us kneel before the LORD our Maker.

PSALM 95:6

When we praise God, our song must be a joyful noise. Spiritual joy is the heart and soul of thankful praise. With humble reverence and holy awe, "let us worship and bow down; let us kneel before the LORD our Maker." This becomes those who know what an infinite distance there is between us and God, how much we are in danger of His wrath and in need of His mercy. We must speak forth, sing forth His praises out of the abundance of a heart filled with love, joy, and thankfulness. We must praise God in concert, in the solemn assemblies; let us join in singing to the Lord.

Because He is our God, not only has He dominion over us, as He has over all the creatures, but He stands in special relation to us. He is our Creator; we must kneel before the Lord our Creator. Idolaters kneel before gods they have made themselves; we kneel before a God who made us. He is our Savior and the author of our blessedness. We are therefore His. We must praise Him because He preserves and maintains us. The gospel church is His flock. Christ is the great and good shepherd of it, and therefore to Him must be glory in the churches throughout the ages.

All the Earth Shall Worship

Say to God, "How awesome are Your works!
Through the greatness of Your power
Your enemies shall submit themselves to You.
All the earth shall worship You and sing praises to You;
they shall sing praises to Your name."

PSALM 66:3–4

In these verses, the psalmist calls upon all people to praise God, "all the earth." This speaks of the glory of God, for He is good to all. The duty of man is that all are obliged to praise God; it is part of the law of creation, and therefore is required of every creature. Next is a prediction of the conversion of the Gentiles to the faith of Christ; the time would come when all the earth would praise God. The psalmist will abound in it himself, and wishes that God might have His tribute paid Him by all the nations of the earth, and not only by the land of Israel. We must be hearty and zealous, open and public, as those who are not ashamed of our Master. And both these are implied in making a noise, a joyful noise. In praising God we must do it so as to glorify Him.

The psalmist had called upon all lands to praise God and foretells that they shall do so. They shall sing to God, that is, sing to His name, for it is only to His declarative glory, that by which He has made Himself known, not to His essential glory, that we can contribute anything by our praises.

The Duty of Praise

Praise the LORD!
For it is good to sing praises to our God;
for it is pleasant, and praise is beautiful.

PSALM 147:1

The duty of praise is recommended to us. We are called to it again and again: "Praise the Lord!" and again, "Sing to the LORD with thanksgiving; sing praises on the harp to our God" (v. 7). Let all our praises be directed to Him and center in Him, for it is good to do so; it is our duty, and therefore good in itself. In giving honor to God we really do ourselves a great deal of honor.

God is the proper object of our praises. Is Jerusalem to be raised out of small beginnings? Is it to be recovered out of its ruins? In both cases, the Lord builds up Jerusalem. The gospel church, the Jerusalem that is from above, is of His building. Are any of His people outcasts? Have they made themselves so by their own folly? He gathers them by giving them repentance and bringing them again into the communion of saints. They are broken in heart, humbled, and troubled by sin, inwardly pained at the remembrance of it. Their very hearts are rent under the sense of the dishonor they have done to God and the injury they have done to themselves by sin. To those whom God heals with the consolations of His Spirit He speaks peace.

God Hears

If I regard iniquity in my heart, the LORD will not hear.
But certainly God has heard me;
He has attended to the voice of my prayer.
Blessed be God, who has not turned away my prayer,
nor His mercy from me!

PSALM 66:18–20

"Now this is strange," said the poor blind man healed by Jesus, "that the miracle wrought upon me has not convinced you, that you should thus shut your eyes against the light." He argues strongly against them, proving not only that he was not a sinner but that he was of God. He argues with great knowledge, though he could not read a letter of the book. He argues with great zeal for the honor of Christ, with great boldness and courage. His argument is somewhat like that of David in Psalm 66:18–20: "If I regard iniquity in my heart, the LORD will not hear me. But certainly God has heard me. . .blessed be God." The formerly blind man speaks the undoubted truth that none but good men are the favorites of heaven, not sinners. God does not hear sinners. This should be no discouragement to repenting, returning sinners, but to those who continue in their trespasses. God will not hear them. But "if anyone is a worshiper of God and does His will, He hears them." A good man is one who worships God and does His will. The unspeakable comfort of such a man is that God hears his prayers and answers them.

Relationships

Brotherly Love

Beloved, if God so loved us,
we also ought to love one another.

1 JOHN 4:11

The Spirit of truth is known by love. The apostle would unite those to whom he wrote in His love, that he might unite them in love to each other. Divine love to the brethren should constrain ours. This should be an invincible argument. Shall we refuse to love those whom the eternal God has loved? We should be admirers of His love, and lovers of His love, and consequently lovers of those whom He loves.

Christian love is an assurance of divine inhabitation. The sacred lovers of the brethren are the temples of God; the divine majesty has a peculiar residence there. Divine love attains accomplishment in us. God's love is not perfected in Him, but in and with us. Faith is perfected by its works, and love has brought us to the love of God, and thereupon to the love of the brethren; for His sake it is therein perfected. How ambitious we should be of this love, when God reckons His own love to us perfected thereby.

One would think that to speak of God dwelling in us, and we in Him, were to use words too high for mortals, had not God gone before us therein. What it fully is must be left to the revelation of the blessed world. But this mutual inhabitation we know, says the apostle, because He has given us His Spirit.

The Least of These

*"And the King will answer and say to them,
'Assuredly, I say to you,
inasmuch as you did it to one of the least
of these My brethren, you did it to Me.'"*

MATTHEW 25:40

Gracious souls are apt to think poorly of their own good deeds, especially as unworthy to be compared with the glory that shall be revealed. Saints in heaven will wonder what brought them there, and that God should so regard them and their services. "We have seen the poor in distress many a time, but when did we see You?" Christ is more among us than we think He is.

"Inasmuch as you did it to one of the least of these My brethren, you did it to Me." The good works of the saints, when they are produced in the great day, shall all be remembered, and not the smallest overlooked, no, not a cup of cold water. They shall be interpreted most to their advantage. As Christ makes the best of their infirmities, so He makes the most of their services.

But what will become of the godly poor, who had no money to help others? Must they be shut out? No, Christ will own them, even the least of them, as His brethren. He will not be ashamed or think it any disparagement to Him to call them brethren. In the height of His glory, He will not disown His poor relations. He will take the kindness done to them as done to Himself, which shows a respect of the poor that were relieved, as well as to the rich that relieved them.

Family Relationships

*Fathers, do not provoke your children,
lest they become discouraged.*

COLOSSIANS 3:21

Here is an explanation of family duties. Wives are to submit themselves to their husbands (v. 18). This is agreeable to the order of nature and the reason of things, as well as the appointment and will of God. It is submission to a husband, and to her own husband, who stands in the nearest relation and is under strict engagements to his own proper duty. This is fit in the Lord. "Husbands love your wives and do not be bitter toward them" (v. 19). They must love them with tender and faithful affection, as Christ loved the church. And they must not be bitter against them, but be kind and obliging to them in all things.

The duties of children and parents: "Children, obey your parents in all things, for this is well pleasing to the Lord" (v. 20). They must be willing to do all their lawful commands, as those who have a natural right and are fitter to direct them than themselves. This is well-pleasing to God. Parents must be tender, as well as children obedient. "Fathers, do not provoke your children, lest they become discouraged." Let not your authority over them be exercised with rigor and severity, but with kindness and gentleness, lest you, by holding the reins too tightly, make them fly out with the greater fierceness.

Mutual Love

Let all bitterness, wrath, anger, clamor,
and evil speaking be put away from you, with all malice.
And be kind to one another, tenderhearted, forgiving one
another, even as God in Christ forgave you.

EPHESIANS 4:31–32

Another caution against wrath and anger, with further advice to mutual love. By bitterness, wrath, and anger are meant violent inward resentment against others, and by clamor, intemperate speeches, by which bitterness, wrath, and anger vent themselves. Christians should not be clamorous with their tongues. Evil-speaking signifies all railing against whomever we are angry with. Malice is that rooted anger which prompts men to design mischief to others. The contrary to all this follows: "Be kind to one another." This implies the principle of love in the heart, and the outward expression of it. Tenderhearted is merciful, to be quickly moved to compassion and pity. Occasions of difference will happen among Christ's disciples, and therefore they must be ready to forgive, therefore resembling God Himself, who for Christ's sake forgive them. Those who are forgiven by God should be of a forgiving spirit and should forgive, even as God forgives. He who does not conscientiously discharge these duties can never fear nor love God in truth and in sincerity, whatever he may pretend to.

Fruits of
the Spirit

The Fruits of the Spirit

But the fruit of the Spirit is
love, joy, peace, longsuffering, kindness,
goodness, faithfulness, gentleness, self-control.
GALATIANS 5:22–23

Paul specifies the fruits of the Spirit that as Christians we are concerned to bring forth in ourselves. He particularly commends love and joy to us, by which we may understand constant delight in God, peace with God, or a peaceableness toward others; long-suffering, gentleness, a sweetness of temper, easy to be entreated when any have wronged us; goodness, readiness to do good to all as we have opportunity; faith in what we profess and promise to others; meekness, not to be easily provoked and, when we are provoked, easy to be pacified; and temperance.

Concerning those in whom these fruits are found, there is no law against them. They are not under law, but under grace, for these fruits plainly show that such are led by the Spirit. This is the sincere care and endeavor of all real Christians. They are now sincerely endeavoring to die unto sin, as Christ had died for it. They have not yet obtained complete victory over it, but they are seeking the utter ruin and destruction of sin in their lives.

The Works of Love

*My little children, let us not love in word or in tongue,
but in deed and in truth.*

1 JOHN 3:18

The example of God and Christ should inflame our hearts with holy love (v. 16). The great God has given His Son to death for us. Surely we should love those whom God has loved, and loved so much.

The apostle proceeds to show us what should be the effect of our Christian love. It must be so fervent as to make us willing to suffer even to death for the safety and salvation of the dear brethren (v. 16). How mortified the Christian should be to this life, and how well-assured of a better! Christian love must be compassionate, liberal, and communicative to the necessities of the brethren (v. 17). Those who have this world's good must love a good God more, and their good brethren more, and be ready to distribute it for their sakes. This love to the brethren is love to God in them, and where there is none of this love to the brethren, there is no true love to God at all. There may be other fruits of this love. Compliments and flatteries do not become Christians, but the sincere expressions of sacred affection and the services or labors of love do.

This love will show our sincerity in religion and give us hope toward God (v. 19). It is a great happiness to be assured of our integrity in religion. The way to secure our inward peace is to abound in love and in the works of love.

Holy Joy

I will greatly rejoice in the LORD,
my soul shall be joyful in my God;
for He has clothed me with the garments of salvation.

ISAIAH 61:10

We are taught here to rejoice with holy joy, to God's
honor. In the beginning of this good work was the
clothing of the church with righteousness and salvation.
Upon this account I will greatly rejoice in the Lord. The
first gospel song begins like this, "My soul magnifies the
LORD, and my spirit has rejoiced in God my Savior"
(Luke 1:46–47). The salvation God wrought for the
Jews, and that reformation which appeared among
them, made them look as glorious as if they had been
clothed in robes of state. Christ has clothed His church
with an eternal salvation by clothing it with the righteousness both of justification and sanctification.
Observe how the two are put together. Those, and only
those, shall be clothed with the garments of salvation
hereafter who are covered with the robe of righteousness
now. Such is the beauty of God's grace in those who are
clothed with the robe of righteousness.

Peace in Christ

"These things I have spoken to you,
that in Me you may have peace.
In the world you will have tribulation;
but be of good cheer,
I have overcome the world."

JOHN 16:33

Jesus comforts the disciples with a promise of peace in Him by virtue of His victory over the world, whatever troubles they might meet within it. "These things I have spoken to you, that in Me you may have peace. In the world you will have tribulation. . .I have overcome the world."

His departure from them was really for the best. It is the will of Christ that His disciples should have peace within, whatever their troubles may be. Peace in Christ is the only true peace. Through Him we have peace with God, and so in Him we have peace in our own minds. The Word of Christ aims at this.

They were likely to meet with tribulation in the world. It has been the lot of Christ's disciples to have more or less tribulation in this world. Men persecute them because they are so good, and God corrects them because they are no better. Between both they shall have tribulation.

But be of good cheer; all shall be well. In the midst of the tribulations of this world, it is the duty and interest of Christ's disciples to be of good cheer; as sorrowful as the temper of the climate, yet always rejoicing, always cheerful, even in tribulation.

Gentleness

Brethren, if a man is overtaken in any trespass,
you who are spiritual restore
such a one in a spirit of gentleness,
considering yourself lest you also be tempted.

GALATIANS 6:1

We are taught to deal tenderly with those who are overtaken in a fault, brought to sin by the surprise of temptation. It is one thing to overtake a fault by contrivance and deliberation, and another thing to be overtaken in a fault. Great tenderness should be used. Those who are spiritual must restore such a person with the spirit of gentleness. The original word signifies to "set in joint," as with a dislocated bone. We should endeavor to set them in joint again, comforting them in a sense of pardoning mercy, confirming our love to them. This is to be done with the spirit of gentleness, not in wrath and passion, as those who triumph in a brother's falls. Many necessary reproofs lose their efficacy by being given in wrath, but when they are managed with tenderness and from sincere concern for the welfare of those to whom they are given, they are likely to make an impression. This should be done with gentleness, "considering yourself lest you also be tempted." We ought to deal very gently with those who are overtaken in sin, because sometime it may be ourselves who need such help. This will dispose us to do unto others as we desire to be done to in such a case.

Unity and Meekness

Endeavoring to keep the unity of the Spirit
in the bond of peace.

EPHESIANS 4:3

This is an exhortation to mutual love. Love is the law of Christ's kingdom, the lesson of His school, the clothing of His family. The means of unity is lowliness and meekness, long-suffering, and forbearing one another in love (v. 2). By lowliness we are to understand humility as opposed to pride; by meekness, that excellent disposition of soul that makes men unwilling to provoke others and not easily be provoked. Long-suffering implies a patient bearing injuries without seeking revenge. The best Christians need to make the best of one another, to provoke one another's graces and not their passions. We find much in ourselves that is hard to forgive, so we must not think it much if we find that in others which we think hard to forgive, and yet we must forgive them. Without these things, unity cannot be preserved. The first step toward unity is humility. Pride and passion break the peace and make all the mischief. Humility and meekness restore the peace. The more lowly-mindedness, the more like-mindedness. The nature of that unity is the unity of the Spirit. The seat of Christianity is in the heart or spirit. It does not lie in one set of thoughts or in one form and mode of worship, but in one heart and one soul.

Long-Suffering

Therefore be patient, brethren,
until the coming of the Lord.
JAMES 5:7

When we have done our work, we need patience to wait for our reward. This Christian patience is not a mere yielding to necessity, as the moral patience taught by some philosophers was, but a humble acquiescence in the wisdom and will of God. Because this is a lesson Christians must learn, though hard and difficult, it is repeated in verse 8: "Establish your hearts"—let your faith be firm, your practice of what is good, constant and continued, and your resolutions for God and heaven fixed, in spite of all sufferings or temptations.

Consider what encouragement there is for Christians to be patient. Look to the example of the farmer. When you sow your corn in the ground, you wait many months for the rains and are willing to wait until the harvest for the fruit of your labor. Consider him that waits for a crop of corn; will you not wait for a crown of glory? If you should be called to wait a little longer than the farmer does, is it not something proportionally greater and infinitely more worth your waiting for? Think how short your waiting time may possibly be. Do not be impatient; do not quarrel with one another. The great Judge is at hand, as near as one who is just knocking at the door.

Brotherly Kindness

Giving all diligence, add to your faith virtue,
to virtue knowledge,
to knowledge self-control, to self-control perseverance,
to perseverance godliness, to godliness brotherly kindness,
and to brotherly kindness love.

2 PETER 1:5–7

Those who want to make any progress in religion must be very industrious. Without giving all diligence, there is no gaining ground in the work of holiness. The believer must have virtue, and then knowledge, temperance, and patience follow. By virtue we mean strength and courage, without which the believer cannot stand up for good works. We need virtue while we live, and it will be of use when we come to die. The believer must add knowledge to his virtue, prudence to his courage. Christian prudence regards the persons we have to do with and the place and company we are in. We must add temperance to our knowledge; be moderate in desiring and using the good things of natural life. Patience must have its perfect work. We are born to trouble and must through many tribulations enter into the kingdom of heaven. To patience we must add godliness. When Christians bear afflictions patiently, they get an experimental knowledge of the loving-kindness of their heavenly Father. We must add brotherly kindness, a tender affection to all our fellow Christians, who are children of the same Father, and therefore to be loved as those who are specially near and dear to us.

Christian Duty

Come Before Him

*Give to the L*ORD *the glory due His name;*
bring an offering, and come before Him.
Oh, worship the Lord in the beauty of holiness!

1 CHRONICLES 16:29

This is a thanksgiving psalm that David, guided by the Spirit, composed to be sung upon the occasion of the public entry of the ark into the tent prepared for it. It is gathered out of several psalms, which some think warrants us to do likewise and make up hymns out of David's psalms, a part of one and a part of another put together so as may be most proper to express and excite the devotion of Christians.

In the midst of our praises, we must not forget to pray for the aid and relief of those saints and servants of God who are in distress. When we are rejoicing in God's favors to us, we must remember our afflicted brethren and pray for their salvation and deliverance as our own. We are members one of another, and therefore when we mean, "Lord, save them," it is not improper to say, "Lord, save us." Let us make God the alpha and omega of our praises. David begins with "Give thanks to the LORD"; he concludes with "Blessed be the LORD" (v. 36).

Gather in His Name

"For where two or three are gathered together in My name, I am there in the midst of them."

MATTHEW 18:20

Assemblies of Christians for holy purposes are here appointed, directed, and encouraged. The church of Christ in the world exists most visibly in religious assemblies. It is the will of Christ that these should be set up and kept up. If there is no liberty and opportunity for large assemblies, then it is the will of God that two or three gather together. When we cannot do what we would in religion, we must do what we can, and God will accept us. The disciples are directed to gather together in Christ's name. In the exercise of church discipline, they must come together in the name of Christ. In meeting for worship, we must have an eye to Christ and communion with all that call upon Him. When we come together to worship God in dependence on the Spirit and grace of Christ, then we are met together in His name. The disciples are here encouraged with an assurance of the presence of Christ: "I am there in the midst of them."

Where His saints are, His sanctuary is, and there He will dwell. He is in the midst of them, in their hearts. It is a spiritual presence, the presence of Christ's Spirit with their spirits, that is intended here. Though only two or three meet together, Christ is among them. This is an encouragement to the meeting of a few.

Judgment Is His

But why do you judge your brother?
Or why do you show contempt for your brother?
For we shall all stand before the judgment seat of Christ.

ROMANS 14:10

Because all of us must shortly give an account, "Why do you judge your brother? Or why do you show contempt for your brother?" Why all this clashing, and contradicting, and censuring among Christians? "We shall all stand before the judgment seat of Christ." Christ will be the judge, and before Him we shall stand as persons to be tried. To illustrate this, Paul quotes a passage out of the Old Testament that speaks of Christ's universal sovereignty and dominion, and that established with an oath: "As I live" (says the Lord) "every knee shall bow to Me" (v. 11). It is a prophecy, in general, of Christ's godhead. Divine honor is due to Him and must be paid. The bowing of the knee to Him and the confession made with the tongue are but outward expressions of inward adoration and praise. *Every knee* and *every tongue*, either freely or by force.

All His friends do it freely. Bowing to Him—the understanding bowed to His truths, the will to His laws, the whole man to His authority; and this expressed by the bowing of the knee, the posture of adoration and prayer. Confessing to him—acknowledging His glory, grace, and greatness—acknowledging our own meanness and vileness, confessing our sins to Him.

Tithing

"Bring all the tithes into the storehouse,
that there may be food in My house."

MALACHI 3:10

Bring in the full tithes to the utmost that the law requires, that there may be meat in God's house for those who serve at the altar, whether there is meat in your houses or not. Let God be first served, and then " 'try Me now in this,' says the Lord of hosts, 'if I will not open for you the windows of heaven.' " The expression is figurative; every good gift coming from above, God will plentifully pour out on them the bounties of His providence. Very sudden plenty is expressed by opening the windows of heaven. Here they are opened to pour down blessings to such a degree that there would not be room enough to receive them. God will not only be reconciled to sinners that repent and reform, but He will be a bountiful benefactor to them. God has blessings ready to bestow upon us, but, through the weakness of our faith and narrowness of our desires, we have no room to receive them. Whereas the fruits of their ground had been eaten up by locusts and caterpillars, God would now remove that judgment. Whereas they had lain under the reproach of famine, now all nations shall call them blessed.

Spiritual
Warfare

Withstand the Evil Day

Therefore take up the whole armor of God,
that you may be able to withstand in the evil day,
and having done all, to stand.

EPHESIANS 6:13

We must be spiritually well armed: "Take up the whole armor of God." Get and exercise all the Christian graces, the whole armor, that no part is naked and exposed to the enemy. Those who would have true grace must aim at all grace, the whole armor. We have no armor of our own that will be strong enough in a trying time. Nothing will stand us in stead but the armor of God.

Our enemies strive to prevent our ascent to heaven. They assault us in the things that belong to our souls. We have need of faith in our Christian warfare because we have spiritual enemies to grapple with; we have need of faith in our Christian work, because we have spiritual strength to call on.

Our duty is to then stand our ground and withstand our enemies. We must not yield to the devil's allurements and assaults but oppose them. If he stands up against us, we must stand against him. To stand against Satan is to struggle against sin, that you may be able to withstand in the day of temptation or any affliction. "And having done all, to stand." Resist him and he will flee. If we move back, he will gain ground. Our present business is to withstand the assaults of the devil and to stand; then our warfare will be accomplished and we shall finally be victorious.

Exceeding Greatness

Far above all principality and power and might and dominion,
and every name that is named,
not only in this age but also in that which is to come.

EPHESIANS 1:21

There is a present inheritance in the saints, for grace is glory begun, and holiness is happiness in the bud. There is a glory in this inheritance, and it is desirable to know this experimentally. It may be understood of the glorious inheritance in heaven, where God does, as it were, lay forth all His riches. Let us endeavor, then, by reading, contemplation, and prayer, to know as much of heaven as we can, that we may be desiring and longing to be there.

It is a difficult thing to bring a soul to believe in Christ. Nothing less than an almighty power will work this in us. The apostle speaks as if he lacked words to express the exceeding greatness of God's almighty power, that power which God exerts toward His people, and by which He raised Christ from the dead. That indeed was the great proof of the truth of the gospel to the world, but the transcript of that in ourselves is the great proof to us. Many understand the apostle here as speaking of that exceeding greatness of power that God will exert for raising believers to eternal life, even the same mighty power which He wrought in Christ when He raised him. And how desirable a thing it must be to become at length acquainted with that power by being raised thereby to eternal life!

Submit in Love

Therefore submit to God.
Resist the devil and he will flee from you.

JAMES 4:7

We are taught to submit ourselves entirely to God. Christians should forsake the friendship of the world and should by grace learn to glory in their submissions to God. We are subjects, and as such must be submissive, not only through fear, but through love. Now, as this subjection and submission to God are what the devil most industriously strives to hinder, so we ought with great care and steadiness to resist his suggestions. "Resist the devil and he will flee from you." If we basely yield to temptations, the devil will continually follow us, but if we stand firm against him, he will be gone from us. Resolution shuts and bolts the door against temptation.

We have great encouragement to act thus toward God (vv. 8–10). Those who draw near to God in a way of duty shall find God drawing near to them in a way of mercy. If there is not a close communion between God and us, it is our fault, not His. He shall lift up the humble. If we are truly penitent and humble under the marks of God's displeasure, we shall in a little while know the advantages of His favor. He will lift us up out of trouble, or He will lift us up in our spirits and comfort us under trouble. The highest honor in heaven will be the reward of the greatest humility on earth.

Ashamed

*"For whoever is ashamed of Me and My words
in this adulterous and sinful generation,
of him the Son of Man also will be ashamed when
He comes in the glory of His Father with the holy angels."*

MARK 8:38

Jesus tells us what men do to save their lives and gain the world. "For whoever is ashamed of Me and My words in this adulterous and sinful generation, of him the Son of Man also will be ashamed." The disadvantage that the cause of Christ labors under in this world is that it is to be owned and professed in an adulterous and sinful generation. Some ages, some places, are more especially sinful, as that in which Christ lived. In such a generation, the cause of Christ is opposed and run down, and those who own it are exposed to reproach and contempt, and everywhere ridiculed and spoken against. There are many who, though they cannot deny that the cause of Christ is a righteous cause, are ashamed of it. They are ashamed of their relation to Christ. They cannot bear to be frowned on and despised, and therefore throw off their profession. There is a day coming when the cause of Christ will appear as bright and illustrious as now it appears mean and contemptible. They shall not share with Him in His glory then, that were not willing to share with Him in His disgrace now.

The Great Commission

Soul-Winners Are Wise

The fruit of the righteous is a tree of life,
and he who wins souls is wise.

PROVERBS 11:30

This shows what great blessings good men are, especially those who are eminently wise, to the places where they live, and therefore how much to be valued. First, the righteous are as trees of life; the fruits of their piety and charity, their instructions, reproofs, examples, and prayers, their interest in heaven, and their influence upon earth are like the fruits of that tree, precious and useful, contributing to the support and nourishment of the spiritual life in many. They are the ornaments of paradise, God's church on earth, for those whose sake it stands. Second, the wise are something more; they are as trees of knowledge, not forbidden, but commanded knowledge. He who is wise, by communicating his wisdom, wins souls, wins upon them to bring them in love with God and holiness, and so wins them over into the interests of God's kingdom among men. The wise are said to turn many to righteousness, and that is the same with winning souls here (see Daniel 12:3). Abraham's proselytes are called the "people whom they had acquired" (see Genesis 12:5). Those who would win souls have need of wisdom to know how to deal with them, and those who do win souls show that they are wise.

The Commission

*"Go therefore and make disciples of all the nations,
baptizing them in the name of the Father and of the Son
and of the Holy Spirit, teaching them to observe all things
that I have commanded you; and lo, I am with you always,
even to the end of the age."*

MATTHEW 28:19–20

The commission Jesus gives to those whom He sent
forth is "Go therefore." This commission is given pri-
marily to the apostles, the architects who laid the foun-
dation of the church. It is not only a word of command
but a word of encouragement: "Go, and fear not; have I
not sent you?" They must go and bring the gospel to the
doors of the nations. As an eagle stirs up her nest and
flutters over her young to excite them to fly, so Christ
stirs up His disciples to disperse all over the world. It is
given to their successors, the ministers of the gospel,
whose business it is to transmit the gospel from age to
age, to the end of the world. Christ, at His ascension, gave
not only apostles and prophets, but pastors and teachers.

What is the principal intention of this commission?
To disciple all nations. "Admit them disciples; do your
utmost to make the nations Christian nations." Christ
the mediator is setting up a kingdom in the world. Bring
the nations to be His subjects. He is setting up a school.
Bring the nations to be His scholars. He is raising an
army. Enlist the nations of the earth under His banner.
The work the apostles had to do was to set up the Christian religion in all places, and it was honorable work. . . .
They conquered the nations for themselves and made
them miserable. The apostles conquered them for Christ
and made them happy.

Nothing Is Hidden

*"Whatever I tell you in the dark, speak in the light;
and what you hear in the ear, preach on the housetops."*
MATTHEW 10:27

Whatever hazards you run, go on with your work, publishing and proclaiming the everlasting gospel to all the world. This is your business; mind it. The design of the enemies is not merely to destroy you, but to suppress that. The disciples must deliver their message publicly, in the light, and upon the housetops, for the doctrine of the gospel is what all are concerned with. The first indication of the reception of the Gentiles into the church was upon a housetop (Acts 10:9). There is no part of Christ's gospel that needs to be concealed; the whole counsel of God must be revealed. Let it be plainly and fully delivered.

The truths which are now hidden as mysteries from the children of men shall all be made known to all nations in their own languages. The ends of the earth must see this salvation. It is a great encouragement to those who are doing Christ's work that it is a work that will certainly be done. This may also be seen as the revealing of the integrity of Christ's suffering servants. However their innocence is now covered, they shall be revealed. All their reproach shall be rolled away, and their graces and services, which are now covered, shall be revealed. Let Christ's ministers faithfully reveal His truths and leave it to Him to reveal their integrity in due time.

Willing Service

For if I preach the gospel, I have nothing to boast of,
for necessity is laid upon me;
yes, woe is me if I do not preach the gospel!

1 CORINTHIANS 9:16

It is the glory of a minister to deny himself that he may serve Christ and save souls. This self-denial yielded Paul much more contentment than his preaching did. This is a duty expressly bound upon him. Those who are set apart to the office of the ministry must preach the gospel. Woe be to them if they do not. But it is not given in charge to all, nor any preacher of the gospel, to do his work without payment. It may be his duty to preach under some circumstances without receiving payment, but he has a right to payment. It may sometimes be his duty to insist on his salary, and whenever he forbears he parts with his right.

Only willing service is capable of God's reward. Leave the heart out of our duties and God abhors them: They are but the carcasses, without the life and spirit of religion. Ministers have a dispensation of the gospel committed to them. Christ's willing servants shall not lack their recompense, and His slothful and unwilling servants shall all be called to account.

What is the reward, then? "That when I preach the gospel I may make it without charge, that I abuse not my power in the gospel." It is an abuse of power to employ it against the very ends for which it is given. And the apostle would never use his power to frustrate the ends of it but would willingly and cheerfully deny himself.

The Road to Damascus

"But rise and stand on your feet;
for I have appeared to you
for this purpose, to make you a minister and
a witness both of the things which you have seen
and of the things which I will yet reveal to you."

ACTS 26:16

Paul asked, "Who are You, Lord?" And He said, "I am Jesus, whom you are persecuting." Paul thought Jesus was buried in the earth and, though stolen out of His own tomb, laid in another. Therefore he is amazed to hear Him speak from heaven, to see Him surrounded with all this glory. This convinced Paul that the doctrines of Jesus were divine and heavenly, not to be opposed but to be cordially embraced, and this is enough to make him a Christian immediately.

He was made a minister by divine authority. The same Jesus that appeared to him in that glorious light ordered him to go and preach the gospel to the Gentiles. What is said about him being an apostle is joined to that which was said to him by the road. He puts the two together here for brevity: "Rise and stand on your feet." He must stand up because Christ has work for him to do: "I have appeared to you for this purpose, to make you a minister." Christ makes His own ministers. He will manifest Himself to all those whom He makes His ministers, for how can those preach Him who do not know Him? And how can those know Him to whom He does not by His spirit make Himself known?

Faithful Service

With goodwill doing service, as to the Lord,
and not to men,
knowing that whatever good anyone does,
he will receive the same from the Lord,
whether he is a slave or free.

EPHESIANS 6:7–8

Christians should be sincere in their obedience, serving with faithfulness. They should have an eye to Jesus Christ in all the service that they perform to their masters, "doing service, as to the Lord, and not to men." Service done to their earthly masters with an eye to Him becomes acceptable service to Him also. They must not serve their masters with eye-service—that is, only when their master's eye is upon them. Their Master in heaven beholds them, and therefore they must not act as men-pleasers. A steady regard to the Lord Jesus Christ will make men faithful and sincere in every station of life. What they do they must do cheerfully, doing the will of God from the heart, serving their masters as God wills they should. This is doing it with goodwill. Service performed with conscience and from a regard to God, though it be to unrighteous masters, will be accounted by Christ as service done to Himself. Let faithful servants trust God for their wages while they do their duty in His fear, "knowing that whatever good anyone does, he will receive the same from the Lord." Though his master on earth may neglect or abuse him instead of rewarding him, he shall certainly be rewarded by the Lord Christ, "whether he is a slave or free." Christ regards not these differences of men at present, nor will He in the great and final judgment.

Anticipating Christ's Return

Our Redeemer

"For I know that my Redeemer lives,
and He shall stand at last on the earth;
and after my skin is destroyed,
this I know, that in my flesh I shall see God."

JOB 19:25–26

There is a redeemer provided for fallen man—Jesus
Christ. The word for *redeemer* is used for the next of kin,
to whom, by the Law of Moses, the right of redeeming
a mortgaged estate belonged. Our heavenly inheritance
was mortgaged by sin; we are utterly unable to redeem
it by ourselves, but Christ is kin to us, our closest kins-
man, and He is able to redeem. He has paid our debt,
satisfied God's justice for sin, and so has taken off the
mortgage and made a new settlement. Our persons also
need a redeemer. We are sold for sin and sold under sin;
our Lord Jesus has worked out a redemption for us and
proclaims redemption to us, so He is truly our redeemer.

Job believes in the happiness of the redeemed and
his own title to that happiness. He knows how the
body is corrupted by the grave but speaks of it without
concern. The same power that made man's body out of
common dust can raise it out of its own dust. He comforts himself with hopes of happiness on the other side
of death and the grave. Soul and body shall come
together again, and the body that must be destroyed in
the grave will be raised again as a glorious body, a spiritual body.

Christ's Dominion

*"Then to Him was given dominion and glory
and a kingdom, that all peoples, nations,
and languages should serve Him.
His dominion is an everlasting dominion,
which shall not pass away,
and His kingdom the one which shall not be destroyed."*

DANIEL 7:14

The kingdom of the Messiah shall be set up in the world, in spite of all the opposition of the powers of darkness. Daniel sees this in a vision and comforts his friends. The Messiah is called the Son of Man here, for He was made in the likeness of sinful flesh, was found in fashion as a man. "I saw one like unto the Son of Man" (see v. 13). Our Savior seems plainly to refer to this vision when He says in John 5:27 that the Father has given Him the authority to execute judgment because He is the Son of Man. Some refer this to His incarnation, but I think it refers to His ascension (Acts 1:9). When the cloud received Him out of the sight of His disciples, it is worthwhile to ask where it carried Him. Here we are told He ascended to His Father and our Father, to His God and our God (John 20:17). He was brought near as our high priest who enters within the veil for us, and as our forerunner. He is represented as having a mighty influence upon this earth. When He went to be glorified with His Father, He had power given Him over all flesh. With the prospect of this, Daniel and his friends are comforted that not only the dominion of the church's enemies will be taken away, but the church's head will have dominion given Him. . . . The church will continue militant to the end of time and triumph to the endless ages of eternity.

Watch and Pray

"But of that day and hour no one knows,
not even the angels in heaven,
nor the Son, but only the Father.
Take heed, watch and pray;
for you do not know when the time is."

MARK 13:32–33

As to the end of the world, do not inquire when it will come, for of that day and that hour, no man knows. It is not revealed by any word of God, either to men on earth or to angels in heaven. But then it says, neither does the Son know. Is there anything which the Son is ignorant of? There were those in primitive times who taught from this text that there were some things that Christ, as man, was ignorant of. They said, "It was no more absurd to say so than to say that His human soul suffered grief and fear." Christ, as God, could not be ignorant of anything, but the divine wisdom which dwelt in our Savior communicated itself to His human soul according to divine pleasure, so that His human nature might sometimes not know some things; therefore Christ is said to grow in wisdom.

"Your duty is to watch and pray. Take heed of everything that would indispose you for your Master's coming; watch for His coming, that it may not be a surprise to you, and pray for that grace which is necessary to qualify you for it, for you know not what the time is, and you are concerned to be ready for that every day, which may come any day."

Citizens of Heaven

For our citizenship is in heaven, from which we
also eagerly wait for the Savior, the Lord Jesus Christ,
who will transform our lowly body that it may
be conformed to His glorious body,
according to the working by which
He is able even to subdue all things to Himself.

PHILIPPIANS 3:20–21

Good Christians, even while they are here on earth, are citizens of heaven. This world is not our home; heaven is. The life of a Christian is heaven, where his home is and where he hopes to be shortly. It is good having fellowship with those who have fellowship with Christ and citizenship with those whose lives are in heaven.

We look for the Savior from heaven, "from which we also eagerly wait for the Savior, the Lord Jesus Christ." We expect His second coming from there. At the second coming of Christ we expect to be happy and glorified there. "Who will transform our lowly body that it may be conformed to His glorious body." There is a glory reserved for the saints, in which they will be instated at the Resurrection. The body is now at best a vile body, but it will be made a glorious body. "According to the working by which He is able even to subdue all things to Himself." . . .Let this confirm our faith of the resurrection, that we not only have the Scriptures, which assure us it shall be, but we know the power of God that can bring it to pass. As Christ's resurrection was a glorious instance of the divine power, so will our resurrection be. And then all the enemies of the Redeemer's kingdom will be completely conquered.

The Trumpet of God

For the Lord Himself will
descend from heaven with a shout,
with the voice of an archangel,
and with the trumpet of God.
And the dead in Christ will rise first.
Then we who are alive and remain shall be
caught up together with them in the clouds
to meet the Lord in the air.
And thus we shall always be with the Lord.

1 THESSALONIANS 4:16–17

"The Lord Himself will descend from heaven with a shout." The appearance will be with pomp and power, with the voice of an archangel. The glorious appearance of this great redeemer and judge will be proclaimed and ushered in by the trumpet of God. The dead shall be raised; the dead in Christ rising first. Those who shall then be found alive will not prevent those who are asleep. They shall be caught up together with them in the clouds to meet the Lord in the air. Here is the bliss of the saints at that day: They shall always be with the Lord. The principal happiness of heaven is being with the Lord, seeing Him, living with Him, and enjoying Him forever. This should comfort the saints on the death of their friends. We and they, with all the saints, will meet our Lord and be with Him forever, no more to be separated either from Him or from one another. The apostle would have us comfort one another with these words (v. 18).

The Appointed Day

But the day of the Lord will come as a thief in the night,
in which the heavens will pass away with a great noise,
and the elements will melt with fervent heat;
both the earth and the works
that are in it will be burned up.

2 PETER 3:10

The certainty of the day of the Lord: That day has not yet come, but it assuredly will come. God has appointed a day, and He will keep His appointment.

The suddenness of this day: It will come as a thief in the night, a time when men are sleeping and secure. The time which men think to be the most improper and unlikely, and when therefore they are most secure, will be the time of the Lord's coming.

The solemnity of this coming: "The heavens will pass away with a great noise, and the elements will melt with fervent heat; both the earth and the works that are in it will be burned up." All must pass through the fire, which will be a consuming fire to all that sin has brought into the world, though it may be but a refining fire to the works of God's hand. What a difference there will be between the first coming of Christ and the second! May we be so wise as to prepare for it, that it may not be a day of vengeance and destruction for us.

Forever and Ever

They shall see His face,
and His name shall be on their foreheads.

REVELATION 22:4

The heavenly state is described as a paradise, a paradise in a city or a whole city in paradise. In the first paradise, there were only two persons to behold the beauty of it, but in this second paradise, whole cities and nations shall find abundant delight and satisfaction.

The river of paradise: Its fountainhead is the throne of God and the Lamb. All our springs of grace, comfort, and glory are in God, and all our streams from Him are through the Lamb. Its quality is pure and clear as crystal (v. 1). All the streams of earthly comfort are muddy, but these are clear, giving life to those who drink of them.

The tree of life in this paradise: Such a tree was in the earthly paradise, but this far excels it. It is situated in the midst of the street, and on either side of the river (v. 2). This tree of life is fed by the pure waters of the river that comes from the throne of God. It brings forth many sorts of fruit—twelve sorts, and it brings forth fruit at all times. There is always fruit on it. The fruit is not only pleasant but wholesome. The presence of God in heaven is the health and happiness of the saints.

This paradise is free from everything evil (v. 3). There is no serpent there, as there was in the earthly paradise. The devil has nothing to do there.

There the saints shall see the face of God. God will own them, as having His seal and name on their foreheads. They shall reign with Him forever. All this shall be with perfect knowledge and joy, walking in the light of the Lord; and this not for a time, but forever and ever.

COMING SOON

TO BARBOUR'S
INSPIRATIONAL LIBRARY
SERIES. . .

A DAILY DEVOTIONAL
BY MATTHEW HENRY

Wisdom for Christian Living

Edited by Toni Sortor

- $4.97
- Leatherette
- 384 pages

Available Wherever Books Are Sold.